Two Are Better Than One

A Guide to Prayer Partnerships That Work

D1449741

Two Are Better Than One

A Guide to Prayer Partnerships That Work

David Mains
and
Steve Bell

Destiny Image Publishers, Inc.®
P.O. Box 310
Shippensburg, PA 17257-0310

"Speaking to the Purposes of God
for this Generation
and for the Generations to Come"

ISBN 1-879050-78-1

For Worldwide Distribution
Printed in the U.S.A.

Published by Destiny Image, Inc.: 1995

Destiny Image books are available through many distributors outside the United States.

Inside the U.S., call toll free to order:
1-800-722-6774

Dedication

To Chapel board member
Carol Beals;
always an encourager
and
a strong prayer warrior.

Contents

Chapter One

How to Grow
Ten Times Stronger

Do you have a friend who will stick by you no matter what? One who will hang in there even if you do something stupid? Or fall into sin? Or go bankrupt? Or are involved in an accident that leaves you crippled? Do you have a spiritual brother or sister who will "be there" if any or all of these things happened?

It was this kind of questioning that prompted a middle-aged, successful businessman in Ohio to begin looking for such a person a number of years ago. Finding a friend like this had a dramatic effect on his life for the good. His family relationships improved. His spiritual walk became

vigorous. New ministry opportunities un-
folded. It was as if a whole new world
opened up to him.

What exactly did he do? What was the
secret he discovered?

That's what this book is about. These
five chapters may be short, but they could
have a giant impact on your life!

The secret Stanley Tam discovered almost thirty years ago (and it's still working!) is that power is unleashed in your life
when you have a prayer partner.

At age seventy-six, Stanley Tam is still
president of United States Plastics, a business with more than 33,000 customers and
which also serves many giant corporations.
Tam remains convinced that "every Christian has a weak side. That's where Satan
always attacks. But if you have a prayer
partner, your weakness will probably be
your prayer partner's strength. The Bible
speaks about one chasing a thousand, and
two putting ten thousand to flight. When
you have a prayer partner, you become ten
times stronger!"[1]

The fact is, praying regularly with
someone else is an easy way to get on track

spiritually. And it doesn't require a major time investment.

This book is for you if:

- You're involved in church, but your spiritual life still seems kind of flat;

- Your prayer experience plateaued some time ago—or maybe it almost stopped altogether;

- You spend little time talking to God (meal prayers excluded) unless a serious problem comes up;

- You know there's a need for a spiritual breakthrough in your life, but you're not sure what it will look like.

Possibly you're a new believer and you've heard older Christians talk about prayer a great deal. But the truth is, you've seldom actually heard anyone pray, except in a more formal way on Sunday mornings. Copying that style has been difficult for you. You really want someone to teach you starting with Lesson One. Even sermons on praying seem a step or two removed from where you are. You want a firsthand experience. You feel like the disciples who said to Jesus, after observing the way He talked to His Father, "Lord, please teach us to pray."

Well, the matter of finding a prayer partner has proven to be a life-changing experience for thousands of believers—the authors included! And it's stimulating. People seldom get drowsy when praying with another person, as sometimes happens when you're alone talking with the Lord.

There are also some long-lasting, positive spillovers with prayer partnerships. For example, when you pray regularly with someone else, you can be confident that it truly affects what happens. God still answers prayer.

Recently my (David) pastor at church preached a marvelous sermon on the value of praying with others. He encouraged us to keep getting together to pray and said it would build our faith. He made the point over and over, "You must understand that God does answer prayer!"

Then he gave current illustrations to encourage us. "Remember several months back, I asked you to pray for the youth of our congregation. We didn't have many young people attending and we were praying that new high school students would come to the Lord. Well, high school students *have* been coming to the Lord...." And then he began to detail what God was doing among the youth at the church.

"Remember how we were praying for wholeness to be restored to certain people? In some lives it was as though all spiritual progress had stopped. Would you believe we're now seeing victory in many of these situations? And I believe it's because you're praying.

"Remember, we were praying for our community—wanting to see the churches begin to work together. That's beginning to happen, too. Next week I'll be preaching at the Lutheran Church. That's a breakthrough! God is responding to our requests. You see, prayer makes things happen!"

On a personal level, in response to requests I've prayed about with my prayer partner in just the past week, I (Steve) have experienced:

- The arrival of some unexpected funds to pay a bill on time.

- Strength through the comment of another to resist a temptation that had been troubling me.

- Input from an out-of-the-blue source which provided me the exact illustration I needed to complete a message and meet my broadcast deadline.

So don't think of praying with someone else as merely spiritual busy work. I have a pastor friend in South Florida with whom I worked for eight years who used to say, "You can do more than pray, but not until *after* you've prayed!"

Another factor when you're praying with someone else on a regular basis—your friend can often give you better perspective regarding both how to pray and how God is answering your requests. There have been times when I (David) prayed with a friend about certain needs, but when God worked I didn't see it. The answer came in a manner unlike what I had in mind. Let me give you an example.

Once I had a suit that was so worn-out you could almost see through it. I needed a new suit, but I also needed to pay my son's college bill. One day my dad came by the office and commented on my suit. "You need a new one, son," he said, "you can almost see through that one! Come along with me. We're going to a store and I'm going to buy you a new suit."

It was a little embarrassing to think that as a grown man I couldn't buy myself a suit whenever I wanted to. It took the input of a prayer partner to point out that God had answered my prayer and that I should be grateful. I had prayed for money from somewhere so I could go and buy a suit on my own. God shortcut the process, but the result was the same. Who was I to complain about how He did it!

I had been a little like Naaman, the Aramaic general described in 2 Kings 5 who wanted God to answer his prayer for healing in a dramatic way. When instead God proposed to heal him through more prosaic means—through washing in the Jordan River seven times—he became angry. "I thought that [Elisha] would surely come out to me and stand and call on the name of the LORD his God, wave his hand over the spot and cure me of my leprosy," he raged (verse 11). It took the wise counsel of his servants to convince him to accept God's way of doing things. "Father," they said, "if the prophet had told you to do some great thing, would you not have done it? How much more, then, when he tells you, 'Wash and be cleansed'!"

That's what a prayer partner can do for you—point out God's hand in a situation where you may not see it.

Another benefit is that relationships reach a whole new level. That's really true! Everyone longs for significant relationships. God wired us that way. Dinah Maria Mulock Craik wrote, "Oh, the comfort, the inexpressible comfort of feeling safe with a person; having neither to weigh thoughts nor measure words but to pour them all out; just as they are, chaff and grain together, knowing that a faithful hand will take and sift them, keep what is worth keeping, and then, with a breath of kindness, blow the rest away." I'm sure this sounds attractive to most everyone.

In Ecclesiastes 4:9-12 we're told, "Two are better than one.... If one falls down, his friend can help him up. But pity the man who falls and has no one to help him up!...Though one may be overpowered, two can defend themselves. A cord of three strands is not quickly broken."

There may be times when you feel alone. You've had a bad phone call. The news was unexpected and came at the worst of times. Now your world is wobbling. You try to pray on your own but God seems far off and incredibly silent. How good it would be to sense His loving touch.

That's possible through an established prayer partnership with as few as one or two others. Rarely will both of you (or the three of you) be struggling in the same areas at the same time. Just meeting together will build up each other. Fresh perspective that provides hope and encouragement is contagious! Everyone benefits when you begin praying regularly with one or two others.

Through involvement in a prayer partnership, you should also improve in your ability to overcome temptation. I (Steve) have continued a prayer partnership for the last couple of years and there has been remarkable change in my friend's ability to resist what has been a long-standing self-destructive pattern. It was a number of months before he divulged his struggle and asked me to help him work his way through it. At his request I became an accountability person. My specific assignment each time we meet is to ask for a progress report regarding his temptation area. Though complete victory has not yet been claimed, significant positive steps have been taken. And the hope for a smashing victory is growing stronger.

Within a short time after entering a prayer partnership, normally you will see improvement in your private time with the Lord. Spending time with someone else in the presence of God enhances personal times with Him. You become practiced and more comfortable in His presence. Talking with the Lord about specific issues in your life no longer seems so abstract. On top of that, many have testified that the promises of Scripture come alive to them in a whole new way. What had become the drudgery of doing basic spiritual disciplines is transformed into a new spiritual vitality.

Finally, the church stands in great need of praying people. Pastors want the prayer support of their members. Those in the congregation have all kinds of heartbreaking requests. Few outsiders come to Christ if nobody is praying for them. And spiritual awakenings always require a prayer base.

In this book we are challenging everyone to move their network of church friendships to a more committed plane. We need to be thinking, *We talk together about any number of things. Why don't we talk to the Lord more?* Such a policy will not become common in the church until people become more accustomed to praying in groups of twos or threes. It's prayer partnerships that will move us toward the day when we feel comfortable, in just about any setting, to stop ordinary conversation and talk instead to the Lord.

It's time we stop thinking of the goal as being one person praying alone for hours in a closet. We need to envision a new day when two or three pray together around the dinner table, in the living room, at the office, as they travel in a car, or wherever they might be.

Prayer in the closet is beautiful, but few do it anymore. So we must envision new pictures of people praying together in all kinds of situations. This type of prayer is not only easier than the closet routine, often it's more powerful. That's the challenge of this book. It's us rediscovering the dynamic of the New Testament church. It's twos and threes coming together with the risen Christ in their midst.

You have a critical decision to make. It could affect you for years to come. What we're suggesting has the potential to convince you of God's supernatural involvement in the everyday issues of life. It may also keep you from making poor decisions which would lead to costly mistakes.

If at present you feel like a novice at praying, that's OK. Things can change—and faster than you think! The best way, the quickest way to get back on track spiritually, is to begin praying regularly with someone else. What we're suggesting could truly be a turning point in your life.

Stanley Tam would agree. Later we'll tell you how he's been a difference-maker for the kingdom who has affected thousands of lives. You can be a difference-maker, too. Promise! And it can all begin with establishing a prayer partnership.

Note

1. See Stanley Tam, *God Owns My Business* (Alberta, Canada: Horizon House Publishers, 1969).

Chapter Two

What Would It Look Like?

It's been going on for a number of years now. These same two businessmen skip lunch every Tuesday, meeting instead in a car to pray. They've seen God answer dozens of requests about their families, their church, their work, and many other issues.

For example, the teenage daughter of one of these men finally broke off an unhealthy relationship with an older college guy. Not only had he never made a profession of faith, he wasn't even nice to her. But it's over. Praise the Lord!

Or another example: they prayed about a conflict in the pulpit search committee for their church. Within the same month both of the problem persons resigned. Now there is unanimity regarding direction, and the committee can get on with its task of finding a new pastor.

Or yet another: the younger of these two businessmen suffered under eighteen months of growing pressures due to the unreasonable expectations of an aloof and demanding supervisor. But now everything's changed. His boss has found the Lord! Suddenly it's as though this praying businessman has a whole new lease on his career and his life.

Because these two friends met faithfully week after week sharing many of their personal concerns, their relationship has grown strong. It's now a deep friendship and they look forward to those power-packed minutes in prayer every Tuesday. Although they skip lunch, they say this time spent together in the presence of the Lord feeds their souls as they help each other find strength in God. The benefits of this mutual relationship far exceed anything either of them anticipated. And would you believe, it all started with a "let's give it a try and see what happens" mentality!

The purpose of this book is to encourage you to establish a prayer partnership with someone else—or with two others if that's more feasible. Even so, understand there's no precise formula guaranteeing that everything will fall in line precisely on schedule. When first getting started you need a "trial and error" attitude. Think of it as an adventure in which you're God the opportunity to direct you into new territories. The process can be exciting, and the ultimate results (once you find that person or persons you're looking for) can be life-changing! You will be tapping into a resource that provides a spiritual strength you never dreamed possible.

Perhaps it would be helpful to picture what some of these prayer relationships look like. Probably none of these scenarios will fit you exactly. Yours will have its own unique features because you will be fashioning an arrangement designed to suit *you*, consistent with who you are as well as fitting your present schedule and lifestyle. But the following may give you some ideas:

• A couple of neighbors used to pray together each Thursday evening. One moved away but they still reserve 7:30 to 8:00 p.m. to pray together. Only now they do it by phone. Despite the distance, they say the format hasn't changed all that much. They're just grateful that the relationship didn't have to end.

• The doors of the church are opened Monday at 6:00 a.m. for a special prayer time and the largest number attending has been four. Usually it's the same three people. But all testify to a special closeness. They say this early Monday meeting is a great start to their week. None of them has any thought of missing it.

• Two high school seniors walk to school together. They've learned that this time can be used to pray. They've become good at it, and adaptable. If someone joins them, they switch easily from talking to God to speaking to the friend who joined them. Praying like this has been a good experience for them. Neither is sure how they will continue the relationship after graduation.

• Saturday mornings are drive time for a father and a son. They usually follow the same route. As they do, they talk over where they are spiritually. Then they take their requests to the Lord. They pray naturally and with their eyes open. When they're finished, they stop for breakfast. Both protect this weekly time because it's grown to be special to them.

• Three single businessmen meet early in the morning at one of their private offices in the city. Usually they get together on Wednesdays, but because all of them travel they've learned to be flexible. Before praying, they spend time listening as one of the group reads from Scripture. These young men keep a record of what they pray about and write down when they sense God has answered their prayers.

• A widower joins an older couple on Friday evenings for prayer. When his wife was still alive, it was a foursome. These friends have walked some difficult roads together. They feel the support of one another and of the Lord. They also pray for a day of national revival. They have a special concern for the new generation coming up. They almost always ask the Holy Spirit to move in the hearts of young people.

• Three homemakers treat themselves to a mid-morning breakfast once a week. They rotate homes. There's a special traveling toy box the kids are allowed to open only at these weekly times. While they are occupied playing, the mothers use their time wisely. They aren't just having fellowship, they're praying together.

Did you see the common thread in these relationships? In each case, these people have:

1) Decided to make prayer a priority.

2) Linked up with a prayer partner (or partners).

3) Mutually agreed on a specific time and place to regularly get together for prayer.

4) Maintained a flexible attitude which allows for adjustments to the unexpected—a move, a trip, a visitor, a schedule conflict, a sick child, even a major illness or death.

Does something like this sound good to you? We hope so. But the great beauty of meeting with another Christian to pray will remain nothing more than a good idea *until you actually find someone to agree to do it with you a time or two*. That's what this book is designed to help you accomplish.

Your Honor, I Object!

It's possible, though, that while you see the great benefits of beginning a prayer partnership, you just can't see how you could fit it into your schedule. You're feeling pressured and overwhelmed as it is. You doubt you could possibly put anything more on your already overflowing plate.

We think it's more than possible, however, that what we're suggesting could be the *answer* to your troubles, not just one more item screaming for attention. Here's what we mean.

Prayer is a paradox that both takes time and frees time. Martin Luther said: "If I fail to spend two hours in prayer each morning, the devil gets the victory through the day. I have so much business I cannot get on without spending three hours daily in prayer."[1] Most of us have never spent three hours in non-stop prayer. But we can understand the principle Luther was underscoring. The greater the demands on our time, the more dependent we are upon the Lord and the more critical it is to spend quality time in His presence. The easiest way to "jump-start" that process is to begin by praying regularly with someone else.

Yes, prayer requires time, but it also frees time. An example could be a problem teenager who is giving you fits. Your attempts to resolve the problems—relying on your own creativity and strength—may be eating up more time than if your prayers allowed God to intervene in the situation. All of the normal fussing and discussing won't change things. But God in His miracle ways can bring about the desired results.

We must never overlook our dependence on God. And how much better to share your burden with a caring partner! Although solutions don't necessarily come overnight (even though they may!), any number of prayer partners will testify that God is incredibly creative in the ways He resolves problems. This must be what Paul had in mind when he instructed us in Galatians 6:2, "Carry each other's burdens, and in this way you will fulfill the law of Christ." If your schedule is full, perhaps a prayer partnership is the one thing you can't afford to do without.

But maybe your objection doesn't relate to a crowded schedule. For some people a common barrier to establishing a prayer partnership is their fear of being vulnerable. They are intimidated by a verse like James 5:16 where we're told, "Confess your sins to each other...." But before you allow this scripture to scare you off, keep in mind that developing this kind of openness and intimacy takes time. It's not the first step in establishing a prayer partnership. Openness should never be forced. It should flow naturally.

What James is writing is not intended to be bad news or something difficult, but is rather a most positive aspect of a healthy, working relationship. James goes on in verse 16, "...and pray for each other so that you may be healed." In other words, what initially may seem intimidating is actually a benefit that only increases in value as your prayer relationship grows.

I (Steve) can testify to this. After admitting honestly my personal struggles and concerns with a prayer partner and then hearing that person pray earnestly about these matters—this does something for me that's invigorating beyond words. I wouldn't give up this aspect of my prayer partnership for anything!

Since we're talking about objections, here's another one. Some people are afraid of praying with someone else because in the past they've had a bad experience. The last thing they want to do is to get involved in a similar situation. But most people who testify to being in a good prayer relationship also admit they've had some bad ones. This didn't stop them—they didn't allow the negative to keep them from the positive. You'd be foolish to quit going to church just because you've had an unsatisfying experience a time or two. And would you give up ice cream because someone once served you a flavor you hated—let's say, cod fish deluxe? We doubt it. And the same should hold true for prayer partnerships.

I (David) was in a small prayer group that met early on Thursday mornings. But it was hard for me because we'd pray from 6:30 to 8:00, at which time I'd rush to the studio to record a broadcast for The Chapel of the Air. It was difficult to shift gears so quickly. Then one of my close friends in the small group died, adding another complicating factor. We had often driven to the meeting together. So I began to pray, "Lord, I need to have a prayer time other than right before I go into the studio to record a program." I made it a simple prayer request.

One day a man stopped by my office. He had just moved into the area. The more he talked, the more I realized he had a longing for national revival, just as I do. "Are you in a prayer group, Dan?" I asked? "Do you ever get together with someone else to pray over the matters you're talking about? If not, maybe sometime we could pray together." He immediately took me up on the idea. He proposed a Saturday morning at 7:30 and we prayed together the next week. Later I invited another friend to join us, and now there are four who meet together every Saturday morning. We have a fantastic time! But the truth is, I stumbled into it only because the former group wasn't right for me.

Yet another common barrier that keeps people from establishing prayer partnerships is that some Christians view prayer as boring. If they want to go to sleep, they pray. Works every time.

That thought may have been in Paul's mind when he wrote in Colossians 4:2, "Devote yourselves to prayer, *being watchful*...." Why would he say it like that? Part of the reason may be that both he and the Lord know we have a tendency to fall asleep when praying (or when listening to a sermon—see Acts 20:7-12. But that's another story). That's where a prayer partner comes in. It's much easier to fall asleep when you're praying alone than when you're praying with a friend.

Logistics is another barrier that might have to be overcome if you are to begin praying regularly with someone else. Life is complicated. People are busy. Often children's schedules have to be considered. But this is true whether you choose to involve your kids in music lessons or in a soccer or baseball league. Juggling is what scheduling is about. For the most part, people learn to make time for what they really want to do.

A number of years back I (Steve) remember feeling convicted about establishing a regular prayer partnership with someone. I needed it and I knew it. But how could I pull it off? I was already getting together with a couple of men for early morning breakfast meetings. But these were more for support or accountability relationships. We weren't praying together in the way we've been describing in this book.

One morning I suggested to one of my friends, "How would you feel about spending some time praying together each time we meet?" He readily agreed. And now, even though we still meet for breakfast, we've cut our eating time short to insure that the last twenty minutes we're sitting in one of our cars praying together. It's working well—and it's wonderful! Making it happen required only a minor adjustment to what was already a part of our routine.

Perhaps you're wondering what you'd pray about. That's sometimes another barrier. The easy answer is to pray about common interest areas. As you meet with your prayer partner you quickly learn what is appropriate and what isn't. Topics might include:

- Family concerns (spouse, children, in-law issues)
- Mutual friends
- Work pressures
- Church matters
- Personal requests (like devotional times, temptation areas, new ministry opportunities, exercise programs, discovering areas of spiritual giftedness, future dreams)
- National revival
- Overseas missions

The possibilities are limitless. What are your needs? The chances are, your friend will share many of them. Those are ideal areas to begin praying about.

Yet another barrier troubling some folks is hypocrisy. They think, *You want me to pray with someone else? I don't even pray alone! I'd be a hypocrite.* Did you know it's much easier to pray with another person that it is to pray alone? When someone becomes a new Christian, it's almost unfair to tell that person to pray every day without first giving him or her a taste of what it's like. If new believers pray consistently with others, before too long they will be strong at praying privately. Having a prayer partner is not for those who are "great saints" as much as for those who need help just getting on track.

Undoubtedly, the biggest barrier relates to whom your prayer partner will be. The perfect person for you might already be in your mind. Then again, it might take awhile to find that individual. Start praying about that even now. Some people testify that it was three months or so before the Lord answered their prayer regarding the identity of their prayer partner. Don't feel as though you have to hurry the process. But do make certain the process is going on. Once the "who" is resolved, it's easier to work on the "when" and "where."

The truth is, if you make this a matter of prayer—that is, the who, the when, the where, and all the logistics involved— sometimes the Lord will answer your requests in a completely unexpected fashion. The person might walk right into your life...or your office!

Stories of people who have become successful in any area of life almost always include how they overcame certain obstacles. Seldom do we arrive at a desired place in life without having to get over a few barriers.

We're encouraging you in this book to reach for a wonderful place, spiritually speaking. Yes, you might have to jump a few hurdles to get there. But it's worth it! To encourage you as you begin that process, pay close attention to the following few pages. They provide helpful work sheets to get you started. It's time to get about the business of developing a plan that will work for *you*!

Note

1. Martin Luther, cited in E. M. Bounds, *Power Through Prayer* (Chicago: Moody Press, 1979), 54-55.

Work Sheet A

Review chapter 2 and note below the common objections to establishing a prayer partnership.

1.

2.

3.

4.

5.

6.

7.

8.

Which of these barriers do you feel *you* need to overcome?

Are there any others not listed? Note below:

Work Sheet B

Of the scenarios mentioned on pages 17 through 20, which seems most appealing to you?

Describe below what you would envision as an ideal situation if you were to establish a prayer partnership with one or two others.

- What day would you meet?

- What time?

- For how long?

- How frequently?

- Where?

Spell out the most desirable qualities you'd look for in the person you would want for a prayer partner. Be as specific as possible.

Work Sheet C

Without doing a lot of introspection, make a short list of the kinds of prayer concerns you'd feel comfortable sharing with someone else:

List below the names of people with whom you already have a good relationship who may be potential prayer partners.

After naming them, perhaps you could rank them in order of preference. Consider comfort level at present, availability, spiritual maturity, etc.

Begin praying (right now!) that God will give you the direction and courage needed to take your next step. After praying, read on.

Chapter Three

How Would We Set It Up?

I (Steve) will never forget the first time I went snorkeling with a spear gun. It was off the coast of Eleuthera, one of the out islands in the Bahamas. I was the leader for a group of students on a short term missions project. Mornings were spent in back yard children's Bible clubs, evenings were reserved for evangelistic services, but afternoons were left open for us to explore the wonders of the island. One such afternoon some locals equipped a few of us to do some spear-fishing.

Assuming we were experienced, they gave us the necessary gear and casually sent us on our way. They assumed wrong. I had no idea what I was doing. But of course

I didn't want to admit this, so with feigned confidence I pushed ahead. "Troops, let's go get ourselves a catch!" I barked. Inside, however, my stomach churned.

Thus began The Great Adventure. Soon I was snorkeling near the reef and "on the hunt." Time passed quickly. When some of my companions left, I assumed they had gotten tired or were hungry. I, however, was not about to quit. I was having the time of my life! Steve Bell was caught up in the ecstasy of teeming ocean life that wiggled and darted before him as he basked in the warmth of clear Caribbean waters. It didn't take me long to become adept at using the spear gun. The bag attached by rope to my waist began to bulge with my catch.

I surfaced and seemed to hear members of my group yelling from shore, "Let's start! Let's start!" Lunchtime? So Soon? *Nah!* I thought, *they can wait a little bit longer. They won't starve if I stay out here a few more minutes.*

Three fish later, I began working my way back to shore so the picnic could begin.

There I was greeted by several very pan-icky friends.

"Why didn't you come in when we were yelling at you?" they demanded. "You could have been seriously hurt! We kept shout-ing, 'Shark! Shark!' "

Shark? What do you mean, "shark"? Do you mean you *hadn't* been yelling, "Let's start"? To submerged ears, they sounded a lot alike—but there's a world of difference. Immediately, a chill coursed through my body despite the warm Caribbean current. My friends hadn't been so anxious to eat as I had thought; what was ravenous was the shark tailing me, attracted by the trail of blood flowing from my prized bag of fish. I had no idea I was about to become a shark's lunchtime entree!

You know what? Before embarking on my spear-fishing adventure I should have used a guide book, a set of instructions, something to help me navigate around the dangers of sharks. This near-miss taught me there are always potential intruders in that part of the Bahamas; but I could have spared myself the experience had I con-sulted an experienced guide.

This chapter is a simple guide to help you navigate around the potential "sharks" of a new prayer partnership. We want you to have a smooth first outing. Though that might happen simply by jumping in and getting started (I still have positive feelings about spear-fishing—though I've never done it again!), it's usually best to go into a new experience having some idea of what to expect. So in case you're feeling hesitant about initiating a prayer partnership, let us help remove the intimidation factor as much as possible.

Here are four suggestions as to what you might cover the first time you get together with someone to pray. These are merely guidelines, some simple ground rules, if you please.

First, it's good to decide up front on how many times you'll meet. We think it makes sense to commit to at least four times to begin with. This should provide ample opportunity to get used to praying together, to get a realistic feel for what a longer commitment would be like, and to work out logistics.

Why four times? Normally, one or two times isn't enough. Of course, there are those special occasions when people immediately "know" they have a good fit. In 1 Samuel 18:1, after David had finished his report to King Saul about slaying Goliath, the text reads, "Jonathan became one in spirit with David...." Theirs was to be an extraordinary friendship between spiritual brothers who hit it off from the moment they met.

More typically, it takes several times together to get a feel for whether you share common interests and burdens. Will your personalities mesh? Do you enjoy meeting together? Is the potential there for openness, caring, and a longer commitment? After getting together four times, you can always decide to continue meeting for as long as you choose.

Also, when trying to start something new, it's usually more comfortable to agree on a starting and ending date. This protects either person from feeling trapped. The more specific the expectations, the greater the possibility for success.

Your four times of getting together to pray should be completed within four to eight weeks. In other words, plan on getting together either once a week or once every other week. Meeting once every three or four weeks makes it difficult to develop any sense of continuity or to build momentum. It's hard to keep up with what's happening in each other's lives if there's too much time between updates regarding answers to your prayer requests. Obviously, when interruptions come, you can always touch base temporarily by way of phone.

Second, when meeting with your prayer partner it's important to withhold judgment about anything that's said. Perhaps this person is facing some difficult personal issues. Serious doubts may have surfaced about God and His involvement in your friend's life. Don't be shocked if your partner blurts out something like, "If we're praying, why doesn't God work faster to fix what's wrong?" or, "What good could possibly come out of all this pain?"

If your partner describes a crisis going on at church or in the home, strong emotions could surface. Out of concern for your friend you might inadvertently say things you'll later regret when you learn more about the situation. Be cautious about adding fuel to the fire. You could be quoted and find yourself in the middle of a situation you know very little about. So keep in mind, there are times when it's best just to listen. Offer words of understanding— "I feel your pain" or, "I hear what you're saying"—without quickly jumping to conclusions. Your basic attitude should be one of acceptance. This is a critical factor in any successful prayer partnership: withhold judgment!

Third, resist the temptation to try to solve the other person's problem, to become a counselor. This is *not* the purpose of joining together. You are meeting to pray. There may even come a point when you need to say, "I believe we've talked enough about this—let's take this concern to the Lord."

As soon as you turn to the Lord, the environment will usually change significantly. Personally, I (David) can sometimes sound negative or unfair when representing a situation to another person. That all changes when I talk directly to the Lord! Naming specifics about a problem with the Lord in the presence of a prayer partner forces me to take a more honest perspective regarding the issue at hand. I also find that intrinsic to praying is a growing sense of faith and hope that usually doesn't characterize conversation between two persons with only the human perspective. So be on your guard! Avoid allowing time set aside to pray to become nothing more than long discussions between friends with a "tack-on prayer" before going your separate ways. That would be self-defeating.

Fourth, everything must be kept in confidence. It is extremely important that trust isn't broken. If confidentiality is lost, not only will it stymie the prayer partnership, the spillover consequences could be devastating. Confidential information in the wrong hands could cause unnecessary pain to a family, eliminate certain ministry opportunities, ruin a reputation, or even destroy a career.

I (Steve) am aware of one situation where a man confided in his prayer partner that he was investigating a new job. The information was passed on. Before he had a chance to discern the Lord's will, word got back to his boss and the man was fired on the spot! Unless it is agreed that the concerns discussed can be shared, confidentiality is non-negotiable in any prayer partnership.

When a prayer partner confides in you, don't even intimate to someone else, "If you only knew the problems somebody I know is going through...." Such comments are never appropriate. If you have to talk about what you've heard, continue speaking with the Lord about it.

These four elements have been put into a Prayer Partners' Covenant at the end of this chapter. It will be helpful for you during your first meeting to go over each of the points of the covenant and sign it together.

Also included as an addendum to this chapter is a suggested agenda for each of your four sessions. Note that they become progressively personal. Feel free, of course, to adjust them in any way that makes you most comfortable.

Structuring Your Meeting Time

Now let's look at some ways to structure your time when you meet to pray. We suggest you divide the total in half so that at least fifteen of the thirty minutes is spent in prayer, or thirty minutes out of the hour.

Don't let the idea of praying for half an hour intimidate you. Most people testify that the minutes they spend in prayer go by much more quickly than you'd think. A couple months back, I (Steve) attended an abbreviated concert of prayer led by David Bryant of the Concerts of Prayer Movement. It was scheduled to last only thirty minutes—usually they're three hours long. The crowd was divided into small groups of threes. When we finished, I assumed thirty minutes had passed. I was amazed to learn that we had been praying nearly an hour!

Another practical suggestion is to allow for a transition between talking *over* prayer requests to talking *directly to* the Lord. This can be done in a number of ways. For example, you might want to take time to read a portion of Scripture. It's always good to review some of the promises of God before speaking with him. A number of appropriate passages are included in this book beginning on page 113.

Or you could review the words of a chorus or hymn. You might even want to sing them together. It isn't necessary to be good musicians to do this. A simple praise song is an excellent way to transition from the horizontal to the vertical, from talking with one another to talking together to the Lord. Possibly this is what Paul had in mind when he wrote to the Ephesian believers (5:19,20), "Speak to one another with psalms, hymns and spiritual songs. Sing and make music in your heart to the Lord, always giving thanks to God the Father for everything, in the name of our Lord Jesus Christ."

Another way to transition is with a minute of silence. This gives you both opportunity to think in quiet about what you want to say to the Lord before you actually begin praying aloud. Barging into God's presence, or beginning to pray too quickly, doesn't allow one's mind to grasp the marvelous truth that the God of the universe is actually listening to your words.

Often I (David) will say to my leadership team when we join together for staff prayer, "Don't anybody talk to the Lord for a least a minute. Take these moments to quiet your heart. Envision Jesus among us. Then think of the most pressing item you want to bring to his attention. Once we've each had opportunity to get that in mind, someone can begin." It's a practical way to focus on the Lord's presence and the priority issues we need to be praying about.

Look at it like this: What would you do if you had an audience with a king or queen or president? Probably you would review ahead of time what items you wanted to cover. You certainly would not want to go into the meeting unprepared. A time of silence can give opportunity for that—a minute or so just to collect your thoughts. Many people say it's helpful to have a small piece of paper to write down notes about what they want to tell the Lord. This way it removes the strain of trying to keep everything in your memory.

Some prayer partners testify to the value of actually kneeling when they start to pray. Kneeling communicates submission. Without saying any words it's a way to give honor to a higher authority. Throughout history it's been traditional for people to kneel in the presence of a king. It's the body language of worship.

Past generations found kneeling helpful both in private and group prayer times. E.M. Bounds in his classic book *Preacher and Prayer* says of William Bramwell, a famous Methodist preacher known for his personal holiness and for many remarkable answers to his prayers, "For hours at a time he would pray. He almost lived on his knees."[1] Of another great man of prayer, Bounds writes, "Payson wore the hardwood boards into grooves where his knees pressed so often and so long."[2]

I (Steve) sense that my generation of Baby Boomer believers has minimal experience of praying on our knees. We like the idea of Jesus as our friend. But reverence and awe in the presence of the King of kings has become all but lost. Perhaps in the days to come we will rediscover the value of kneeling when we pray. By this we say to the Lord, "You are worthy to be praised. You are our ultimate authority. We are privileged to be your humble servants. What an honor it is that you are willing to act on our behalf!"

Most of all, before you pray it's mandatory to remind yourselves that God is truly listening. Otherwise, like anything else, prayer can become routine. If you're not careful, it ends up being merely a human exercise done with closed eyes.

The great beauty of praying with someone else is that the togetherness tends to help resolve this problem. Hearing others speak to the Lord is an evidence of their sincerity, their faith, and their belief. Their words underscore in your mind and heart the same awareness that God is listening attentively.

Sometimes when you get used to praying with other people, you can forget that God is present. So keep this marvelous truth in mind. Throughout all generations Christ has been true to His promise, "For where two or three come together in my name, there am I with them" (Matthew 18:20).

During the actual time of prayer, it's important to remain as conversational as possible. When talking with a friend, it's annoying if you say a few words and before you can speak again, you have to listen for four or five minutes. Praying with a partner is the same way. If one person prays for a long time, and you have opportunity to interject only a thought or two before he takes over again—that's no good. The general rule should be, "Pray as often as you want, but pray in short paragraphs or sentences." Pray until a given topic has been covered and everyone says all he or she wants to, then move on to the next subject.

Finally, don't feel that pauses in prayer have to be filled with talk. Pauses mark normal conversation; they should be a part of prayer conversation as well. When driving somewhere with another person, you don't feel obligated to talk all the time. There's no rule that says every silence in a car must be filled. There's no rule like that for prayer times, either.

Sometimes pauses are opportunities for people to gather their thoughts. Pauses can also provide the Holy Spirit a quiet moment to communicate a word from the Lord to a person's inner soul.

When there's a pause, a prayer partner can say, "Let's stop talking to the Lord for a minute because I need to clarify something." Then after the matter has been explained and is better understood, simply go back to praying.

Summary

Let's go over once more the guidelines we are suggesting when you get together with someone else to pray:

- Decide how many times you'll meet and how often.

- Withhold judgment regarding anything said.

- Resist the temptation to become a counselor—your partner's problems are not yours to solve.

- Maintain confidentiality.

- At your first meeting, review the covenant on page 53 and sign it.

- Try to spend at least half your time together actually praying.

- Allow for a transition time to shift from the horizontal to the vertical. You could:
  - Read Scripture
  - Review the words of a song or sing it
  - Allow for quiet to gather your thoughts
  - Consider kneeling together
  - Remind yourself that God is truly listening
- Keep prayer times conversational.

- View pauses as a normal and positive ingredient of your times together.

Is it clear by now what we mean by a prayer partnership? Does it look like something you'd like to try? We believe you'll be amazed at the almost immediate benefits. Why not give God an opportunity to work in your life through this means?

And don't put this book down just yet. While you're still motivated, go on to the following pages designed to help you figure out where to go from here.

Notes
1. E.M. Bounds, *Preacher and Prayer* (Grand Rapids, Mich.: Zondervan Publishing House, 1950), 42.
2. Ibid., 41.

Prayer Partners' Covenant

We are joining in a prayer partnership

from _____ to

(date)

_____ .

(date)

We agree to:

- Meet at least four times.

- Withhold judgment on problems or doubts communicated by our partner. Our attitude will be one of acceptance.

- Avoid the temptation to try to solve each other's problems during these sessions. Our purpose for meeting is primarily to pray.

- Keep everything said at these meetings completely confidential. We must be able to trust each other if we are to develop openness between us.

Signed, _____

_____

_____

Suggested Agenda to Initiate a Prayer Partnership

Session 1

1. Read aloud and sign the Prayer Partners' Covenant on page 53.

2. Ask each other, "How can I pray for you in the next week or two?" Consider matters such as health, family, work, important decisions, areas of discouragement, and so on. Keep notes on these prayer requests.

3. Pray together, asking the Lord to use this prayer partnership to help you grow in your spiritual life.

Session 2

1. Review the covenant. Have you abided by it?

2. Go back over the prayer requests you made last time. How has God answered your prayers?

3. Discuss new prayer concerns. Focus especially on any spiritual needs you may have. Ask each other, "How are you doing right now spiritually? How can I encourage you in prayer?"

4. Make notes and pray for each other along those lines.

Session 3

1. Review your previous requests. How has God answered your prayers? What has he been teaching you in recent weeks?

2. Discuss any new prayer requests. Focus especially on your church. Ask each other, "What would you most like God to do in your/our congregation?" Remember, this is not a time for debate or lengthy discussion. Merely make known your requests, and take them to the Lord.

3. Pray with each other about your personal concerns, your spiritual growth edge, and your hopes for your church.

Session 4

1. Review the prayer requests of past sessions. Talk about how God has answered your prayers.

2. Make known any new prayer concerns. As you think over the last several weeks, ask each other, "What is one new thing you'd like to see happen in your relationship with God?"

3. Pray together.

4. Now that you've met four times, talk about whether you might continue this prayer partnership. If you decide to go on, you may even want to invite one or two others to join you.

Chapter Four

What Will It Accomplish?

"It wasn't that hard."

"I found it easy to pray together almost as soon as we began."

"The difficulties I anticipated were more in my mind than anywhere else."

"I should have done this sooner!"

That's a representative sample of the comments we hear from Christians who for the first time have tried prayer partnerships. Possibly you're already finding out how helpful a prayer partner can be. You look forward to your times together—they are invigorating spiritually. You sense a deep friendship forming, maybe even a long-term relationship.

So now might be a good time to take a look at the benefits that accrue over the long haul once a partnership has been established. So far we have only suggested that you get together with someone else at least four times. But we hope it will be such a positive experience that you'll want to continue the relationship.

Meeting to pray with another Christian should give you a taste of something that's so good you'll want to continue it in the months and years ahead. Wouldn't it be something if what you initially intended to be a four-times-only experiment turned into a four-month-long or four-year-long discipline—or better yet, a lifetime one?

The truth is, praying regularly with someone else has become a life pattern, a positive habit, for a number of dynamic Christians. Many believers, spiritually eager and determined to make a difference in their worlds, testify that they couldn't imagine taking on all they do without the support of a prayer partner. You might not yet be at such a place—but perhaps someday!

Christian businessman Stanley Tam waited until his mid-forties to form a prayer partnership. Now he's been at it weekly with his friend, Art, for nearly thirty years. Proverbs 27:17 tells us, "As iron sharpens iron, so one man sharpens another." Their continuing prayer times have given birth to such endeavors as a Bible class at Tam's United States Plastic Corporation plant. It was a neutral place where non-believers felt comfortable to attend and study the Word of God. Over the years more than one hundred employees have accepted Christ as Savior through that class.

Another outreach ministry sparked by their weekly prayer times was putting up tract racks in area self-service laundromats. Currently there are nineteen locations. Through this effort nearly one million gospel tracts have been distributed, resulting in many people making decisions for Christ.

WTGN, a Christian radio station in Lima, Ohio, also came into being via the weekly prayer partnership of these two men. Since its beginning, the Lord has used the station to minister to hundreds of thousands of people. All of this and much

more was begun because two men determined to get together regularly to pray,
and along with the mutual strength and
encouragement they found, they also dared
to dream...and then act!

What if they never had the courage to
get started? Or what might God have accomplished through them if they had
started fifteen or twenty years earlier? The
point is, there is a cumulative impact for
Christ and His Kingdom as believers join
together to seek the face of their Lord.

If praying with someone is new terri-
tory for you, here's one benefit you won't
want to miss. Keep a record of your requests and record how God answers them.
A sample sheet for your use is found in this
book on page 101.

You'll be amazed at how good the Lord
is. It's always more enjoyable to talk together about what's happened than merely
to process individually what God has done.
This suggestion isn't too unlike the "stones
of remembrance" God instructed Joshua to
set up following the crossing of the Jordan
River. Joshua 4:6b-7 records Joshua's words
to his fellow Israelites:

In the future, when your children ask you, "What do these stones mean?" tell them that the flow of the Jordan was cut off before the ark of the covenant of the LORD. When it crossed the Jordan, the waters of the Jordan were cut off. These stones are to be a memorial to the people of Israel forever.

Remembering God's goodness has always been a priority for His people throughout history. Songs or psalms were written so people wouldn't forget what God had done. Psalm 107 is an example:

Give thanks to the LORD, for he is good; his love endures forever. Let the redeemed of the LORD say this...

What follows is a litany of specific deeds God performed on behalf of His people. Repeatedly throughout the psalm this phrase is found: "Let them give thanks to the LORD for his unfailing love and his wonderful deeds for men..." (verses 8,15,21,31). Both experience and scripture passages like this teach us that keeping a record of specific ways God answers our prayer requests is an excellent way to build our faith.

Another plus about praying regularly with someone else over a period of time is that along the way surprises occur. For example, one person we know said he always had trouble praying for missions. He wasn't that informed on the topic so he struggled trying to be specific. On one occasion as he listened to a partner praying for various missionaries around the world, it was almost like going on a spiritual travelogue. The missions novice was saying quietly, "Just keep praying. This is wonderful. I'm with you. Don't stop. I've never heard this kind of praying before. Go on to the next country."

Sometimes when you read a story or see a film, you almost wish you were part of the action. It's more exciting than your everyday world. This may well be one of the additional surprises that comes from a prayer partnership. You begin to feel as though you're a part of the ongoing story of the expanding kingdom of Jesus Christ. You sense yourself living in the reality of the New Testament, being brothers and sisters with the apostles of old. This is really true! Numbers of people have made comments to us such as:

"For the first time I see how I'm part of something bigger than just my own needs."

"I never, ever remember hearing anyone pray for our denomination before. And the compassion in her voice convicted me of my indifference."

"I've started reading some of the missionary material I get in the mail. That's directly a result of my prayer partnership."

"The new person in our group had a list of ten people on what he called his 'Most Wanted' list. These were non-Christians he was praying for. He thanked the Lord for one on his list who had just come to Christ. I felt convicted that I had never prayed for anyone like this."

"I never used the term 'miracle' before. But I heard my prayer partner ask the Lord for a miracle in this impossible situation. And it happened! All of a sudden I felt I was back in Bible times."

Many Christians who have been in prayer partnerships for long periods of time speak of the benefits that spill over into their relationships and responsibilities at church. One is the increasing comfort they feel about praying spontaneously with others. Before they were too intimidated, almost immobilized. They couldn't bring themselves to say to someone, "Why don't we pray about that right now?" Now they're experienced and confident enough to do it anytime.

In phone conversations they readily suggest, "Before we hang up, let me pray for you. Your need is legitimate. You have reason to be concerned. Let's take it to the Lord."

When someone at church asks for prayer, they don't just say, "I'll be praying for you," and let the matter drop. Rather, they respond, "Let's find a spot over there in the corner and I'll pray for you right now. That way you'll get a feel for how I promise I'll be praying for you during the days ahead."

Sometimes committee meetings or leadership meetings of the church are difficult.

Typically they begin or end with prayer. But along the way, as hard issues arise, it can be good to have someone say, "Would you mind if we took a moment right now to pray about what's happening? I feel it would be more helpful for all of us if we could sense the presence of the Lord in this situation." Then after prayer, everyone present should be better able to hear Christ's voice in what is said. Wisdom to know the difference between what is good and what is best can emerge. As basic as it sounds, the insertion of prayer can often be the most effective way to find solutions to difficult situations.

Is it being too bold or too pushy to suggest to people who have mentioned a prayer request, "Let's stop right now and pray about that matter"? Might some people resent being prayed for on the spot? The answer is almost always "no!" In fact, both of us can point to numerous times when we prayed for someone and looked up to see tears in the person's eyes. Each of us has heard comments like, "Thank you so much. I've never had anyone do that for me before. You can't imagine what an encouragement your interest in my problem is. I'm deeply touched that you actually took the time to pray with me." Other times no words were spoken, but an embrace, a spontaneous gesture of gratitude, said volumes.

What we're reporting isn't unique to us. Many believers have experienced what we're describing. You may be one who could describe similar incidents. If not, would you like to be such a person? Does this kind of ministry—encouraging those who are hurting and in need—sound attractive to you? It's not that complicated to bring hope to someone through prayer. *Getting involved in a prayer partnership and staying with it trains you to be such a person.*

The body of Christ should function like this. Unfortunately, we've developed a dysfunctional pattern in many churches. You've heard about dysfunctional families— families that don't operate the way they should. The same symptoms of dysfunctional families often plague the church family.

Dysfunctional families are marked by denial and delusion. They won't admit they have problems. Maybe a father is alcoholic, but family members won't talk about it. They've learned to avoid that conversation because it's too painful. Perhaps a mother uses her migraine headaches as a means of manipulating people to do what she wants. "I don't want to talk, my head hurts too much. Just do what I say!" No one suggests that she go to a doctor for help. They get used to the problem and try to live with it as best they can.

In the church family, people also have problems they don't talk about. We know that people who come to the Lord aren't sanctified instantly, yet in the church very few people talk about their problems. We don't know that this individual struggles with lust, or that one with greed. Maybe the man over there has a bad temper. We all agree that everyone is a sinner, but we don't know what anyone's specific "besetting sin" is, except for those which are more blatant.

One of the reasons for this is that it's difficult for us to be open about our problems during a Sunday morning service. It's even hard for that to happen during a weeknight church prayer meeting. Typically, the format of such gatherings isn't adequate to accommodate this kind of open communication.

That's where prayer partnerships can be so beneficial. Especially if they continue over a period of time. The relationship builds. There's a growing sense of oneness and mutual trust. The persons involved feel more comfortable with each other and increasingly speak openly and honestly about their real needs and struggles. They support each other in prayer when they go their separate ways. The result? Spiritual growth. A renewed realization that God answers prayer. They draw strength from one another. They encourage one another and continue to build up each other. As they draw closer to the Lord, the Spirit of God energizes them for service.

Believers involved in effective prayer partnerships typically become positive forces in their local church. Their growing belief in the power of prayer tends to filter into other areas of the congregation. Their enthusiasm about prayer becomes contagious. From their example, others catch on and begin the practice of saying, "Why don't we stop right now and pray about that?"

Fortunately, in every church there are many long-standing friendships. These relationships are already in place in all congregations. Unfortunately, too often these friends who have a comfort level with each other don't pray together. They haven't learned to say, "It's been a good evening together. But before leaving let's spend some time praying for our pastor, the services this weekend, the youth outreach, whatever." By establishing prayer partnerships, this desperately needed aspect of church life could develop most naturally.

Prayer is the natural language of the church. Over a period of time all who are a part of the church should become fluent at speaking it.

Ten years ago my wife and I (Steve) were asked by some missionaries in Peru if we would serve as legal guardians for their two daughters who were being sent to school in the States. We readily agreed and it's been a wonderful experience for our family. These girls have been the sisters our two boys never had.

Faith, the younger of the two and now a college graduate, still lives with us. Both she and her sister, Sharon, grew up speaking Spanish. But they've also mastered English. Our boys are fascinated that the girls are equally fluent in both languages. "Which one do you think in?" they ask. "It depends on who's speaking to us," the girls answer.

The language of the church is prayer. And shouldn't believers master the ability to easily shift back and forth from everyday conversation to talking with the Lord? Like Faith and Sharon and others who are bilingual, believers need to feel comfortable with earthly talk and heavenly talk and with moving naturally from one language to the other. In fact, for the church to grow strong again, believers must determine to make prayer their second language. Otherwise we'll end up little more than secular Christians who have written the supernatural out of our everyday lives.

If we confine prayer to strictly formal occasions, we may be on the verge of what

Jesus talked about in Matthew 15 when He quoted Isaiah the Prophet: "These people honor me with their lips, but their hearts are far from me" (verse 8).

Most pastors feel (and probably rightly so) that their churches are weak in the area of prayer. The gauge they use is attendance at the weekly prayer meeting. Maybe it would be good to change the measuring stick. The standard we're suggesting is, "What are the prayer partnerships like throughout the congregation?" If those are strong, the church prayer base will solidify and will most likely affect the weekly prayer meeting.

Why? Because so much more can be accomplished in prayer partnerships. They are more personal. They provide a much greater sense of accountability than can be found in a large prayer gathering.

That's not to minimize the value of a large prayer meeting. We need both. But considering where the church is at present, it's our conviction that Christians need to rediscover the great value of praying regularly with one or two others. Prayer partnerships have been overlooked for too long.

Paul reminds the church at Ephesus that our heavenly Father "is able to do immeasurably more than all we ask or imagine, according to His power that is at work within us, to Him be glory in the church...." (Ephesians 3:20,21).

Let's allow that glory to begin to show itself to you and a faithful prayer partner. Then let's watch it expand to the church at large. And let us eventually see it bring glory to "Christ Jesus throughout all generations [including ours!], forever and ever! Amen."

Chapter Five

Maranatha!

The serious problems of our society have caused some people to feel that our culture is in the process of unraveling. In the past few decades we've gotten used to divorce, drunkenness, profanity, drug trafficking and its related crimes, pornography, murder, gambling, homosexuality, abortion, child abuse, the occult, incest, Satan worship, and the list goes on.

Many concerned church leaders have issued a call for concerted prayer. In the past such a challenge often resulted in marvelous times of awakening. In 1794, twenty-three new England ministers wrote a letter calling for God's people to intercede

on behalf of the nation. Circulated throughout the churches, it asked for:

> Public prayer and praise, accompa-
> nied with such instruction from God's
> Word, as might be judged proper, on
> every first Tuesday, of the four quar-
> ters of the year, beginning with the
> first Tuesday of January, 1795, at
> two o'clock in the afternoon...and so
> continuing from quarter to quarter,
> and from year to year, until, the good
> providence of God prospering our en-
> deavors, we shall obtain the blessing
> for which we pray.[1]

The response of God's people was overwhelming. Many Christians became a
part of "Aaron and Hur Societies." That
title refers to the Old Testament story
where Moses' arms were held up by these
two friends of his. The Israelites won the
battle in the valley below as long as up on
the mountain Moses' arms remained
lifted—that was the job of Aaron and Hur.
In the same way, these eighteenth-century
men and women committed themselves to

serious prayer on behalf of their pastors and spiritual leaders.

It was surprising how quickly the Lord responded to the mounting pleas of his people. The Second Great Awakening, coming during the presidency of John Adams, was fanned by spiritual fires burning brightly in churches all through the East. Schools such as Yale, Princeton, Harvard, Dartmouth, and Amherst witnessed numbers of conversions, with many of these young people eventually going into mission work.

In what was then the West, thrilling stories were told about revival camp meetings in states such as Ohio, Pennsylvania, Kentucky, and Tennessee. Recently I (David) visited Cane Ridge, Kentucky. I remember what Fred Hoffman wrote about events there in his book, *Revival Times in America*.

> Rev. B.W. Stone, a Presbyterian minister in Bourbon County, Kentucky, hearing of the wonderful works of God in Logan County, traveled across the state early in 1801 to see for himself what God had wrought. Upon his return to his own parish,

his account of the things he had seen and heard made such a powerful impression upon his people that within a few weeks a similar revival broke out in that field, at Cane Ridge, which became one of the influential awakenings in this whole period. Writing of the events of those days, Mr. Stone relates:

A memorable meeting was held at Cane Ridge in August 1801. The roads were crowded with wagons, carriages, horses and footmen moving to the solemn camp. It was judged that between twenty and thirty thousand persons were assembled. Four or five preachers spoke at the same time in different parts of the encampment without confusion. The Methodist and Baptist preachers aided in the work, and all appeared cordially united in it.

There were of one mind and soul.... We all engaged in

singing the same songs, all united in prayer, all preached the same gospel. The number converted will be known only in eternity. Many things transpired in the meeting which were so much like miracles that they had the same effect as miracles on unbelievers. By them many were convinced that Jesus was the Christ, and were persuaded to submit to Him. This meeting continued six or seven days and nights, and would have continued longer, but food for such a multitude failed. To this meeting many had come from Ohio and other distant parts. These returned home and diffused the same spirit in their respective neighborhoods, and similar results followed.[2]

In his book *The Eager Feet: Evangelical Awakenings, 1790-1830*, Dr. J. Edwin Orr writes:

The crucial test of the genuineness of the 1800 Awakening was not the size of the crowds or the degree of excitement, but the spiritual fruits. Dr. George A. Baxter affirmed:

> On my way I was informed by settlers on the road that the character of Kentucky was entirely changed, and that they were as remarkable for sobriety as they had formerly been for dissoluteness and immorality. And indeed I found Kentucky to appearances the most moral place I had ever seen. A profane expression was hardly ever heard. A religious awe seemed to pervade the country.
>
> Upon the whole, I think that the revival in Kentucky the most extraordinary that has ever visited the Church of Christ.[3]

Another refreshing, major move of the Spirit occurred throughout North America in 1857 and 1858. It began in a small,

Wednesday noon prayer meeting held at the Fulton Street North Dutch Church in New York City. This time it wasn't pastors who spearheaded the move, but a businessman by the name of Jeremiah Lanphier. Throughout the city Lanphier distributed a handbill inviting "merchants, mechanics, clerks, strangers, and businessmen generally an opportunity to stop and call upon God amid the perplexities incident to their respective avocations. It will continue for one hour; but it is also designed for those who may find it inconvenient to remain more than five or ten minutes."[4]

He scheduled his first prayer meeting for noon on September 23, 1857. At five past the hour no one had responded to his invitation. Ten minutes passed, then fifteen. Lanphier was still alone. He began to pace, hoping (and praying!) his labors were not in vain. Twenty minutes passed, then twenty-five. Finally, at 12:30, Lanphier's first "prayer partner" appeared. Soon four others joined them and the prayer meeting began. The next week forty people arrived ready to pray and it was decided to hold daily rather than weekly meetings. Six months later, ten thousand businessmen were meeting each day for prayer in New York City. According to Orr in his book *The Light of the Nations*,

> Undoubtedly the greatest revival in New York's colorful history was sweeping the city, and it was of such an order to make the whole nation curious. There was no fanaticism, no hysteria, simply an incredible movement of the people to pray.[5]

Gaining momentum, it spread rapidly all across the country. So many people wanted to pray together at noon that the churches weren't able to hold everyone. In one major city after another, fire departments, theaters, and business offices were opened to accommodate the crowds. At high tide it's estimated that 50,000 a week were being converted.

The book *America's Great Revivals* details some of what was happening outside of New York:

> In a church in the Midwest twenty-five women got together once a week to pray for their unconverted

husbands. The pastor traveled to the Fulton Street meeting to testify that on the Sunday he had left the last of the twenty-five husbands had been received into the church.

At the very first union prayer meeting held in Kalamazoo, Michigan, someone put in this request: "A praying wife requests the prayers of this meeting for her unconverted husband, that he may be converted and made an humble disciple of the Lord Jesus."

At once a stout, burly man arose and said, "I am that man. I have a pious, praying wife, and this request must be for me. I want you to pray for me." As soon as he sat down, another man got up and said, "I am that man. I have a praying wife. She prays for me. And now she asked you to pray for me. I am sure I am that man, and I want you to pray for me."

Three, four or five more arose and said, "We want you to pray for us too." That started a revival that brought at least 500 conversions.[6]

Presbyterian revivalist Charles Finney, still alive at the time, commented, "There is such a general confidence in the prevalence of prayer, that the people very extensively seemed to prefer meeting for prayer to meeting for preaching. The general impression seemed to be, 'We have had instruction until we are hardened; it is time for us to pray.'"

The truth is there has never been a time of awakening without a strong prayer base. Revival hinges on this issue. Unfortunately, most congregations today are weak when it comes to naming people who fit under the "prayer warrior" heading.

Were you aware that once again a call to prayer for spiritual awakening is being issued? Many church leaders are saying that this is our society's only hope. How encouraging that large concerts of prayer are now being held in numbers of cities throughout the states and provinces! People from many denominations are joining together in crowds sometimes as large as 7,000. These prayer rallies last as long as three hours.

In places such as the Pacific Northwest and in New England, many ministers are starting to meet together weekly for prayer. The gatherings cross denominational lines, racial lines, even Catholic/ Protestant lines. It's hard to measure, but we believe there's also a core of committed people who are fasting and praying that once again we will soon see another powerful moving of the Spirit.

Usually when people respond to a major call to prayer like this, it's only a period of three to five years before the revival comes in full force. If it hasn't happened by then, the interest in prayer is difficult to sustain and the movement loses its momentum. So we are in a special window of time when everything possible needs to be done to mobilize that great army of prayer.

Most believers, however, are weak in this area. They want to be part of what is happening, but they don't know how to accomplish it. Can a miracle happen? Can they become spiritual prayer warriors overnight?

We say that prayer partnerships are the easiest way to bring this about!

Forming prayer partnerships is not important just because of you and your needs. Yes, praying together with a friend for a number of years will have tremendous value. But for the sake of a holy movement needing additional fuel, get a prayer partnership started and then be open to inviting one or two others to participate with you. With even four getting together, there's still adequate time to cover personal prayer needs, and the added personalities each seem to have something special to contribute to the mix. Four also gives the opportunity to divide and begin two new groups; or maybe, at a certain time, all four will look for new partners. Then the ministry is quadrupled. The church needs to discover how to multiply quickly by dividing!

What we are saying is that it would be far too limiting to view your prayer partnership as having significance only for your personal needs. We've been called to live under the reign of Jesus. We are a part of His Kingship or Kingdom. We want His name elevated around the world. A part of growth in the area of prayer is not only to pray the desires of each partner, but also to pray the desires of the King who joins you when you gather in His name.

That's why in His model prayer, Jesus included these words: "Thy Kingdom come, Thy will be done on earth as it is in Heaven." This was so we would place His wishes alongside our own, that there would be a proper balance.

In a way, it's like saying to Jesus, "Here are our desires, we've written them down. Now, Your Majesty, what requests would you have us put on this list?"

To us it seems likely Christ would say something like, "I very much want to see a movement of my Spirit through the churches in the land. Too many congregations are like the church at Ephesus. There's a lot that's good about them, but they've lost their first love (Revelation 2:7). Other churches are like Sardis. To them I want to say, 'Wake up! (Revelation 3:2). Don't you understand what is happening in your culture? My army needs to hear my trumpet playing reveille!' "

Reveille/revival...the words mean about the same thing. It's time to stop sleeping and get involved once again in the battle!

> Wake up, O sleeper, rise from the dead, and Christ will shine on you (Ephesians 5:14b).

How many churches are like the one at Laodicea where Christ was knocking on the door and wanting in? That passage in Revelation 3:20 has been used to help encourage people to invite Christ into their hearts. But it really is about Jesus knocking on the door of a church. What an incredible picture! It's Christ knocking on the front door of a sanctuary saying, "If you'll just let me in, we could have wonderful fellowship. Make your decision. Either I'll enter and be an integral part of what's going on, or I'll leave."

Don't we all want Him to come in? We want Christ to make His presence known in the church in a remarkable way, and we want the church to again be the salt that keeps society from rotting. The outstanding characteristic of all times of genuine revival is an overwhelming sense of the presence of the Lord. Nothing could be better than to have our Lord make known His wishes for the church. In the pages that follow you will find a place to write down what you perceive Christ's prayer requests might be.

This is the ultimate result of our challenge to prayer partnerships. It's thrilling to see personal needs being met, but how much greater to want the Lord's desires granted also! It may be that although you initially got involved in a prayer partnership in order to see your own needs met, you will suddenly find yourself involved in a sweeping movement of the Spirit orchestrated by Christ Himself. Do you think that would be disappointing? No way! Impossible!

In Scripture we are taught to pray for the return of Christ. That's what the word *maranatha* means: "Amen. Come, Lord Jesus" (Revelation 22:20). Can we also learn to pray together for the coming of Christ in new power and love in relationship to the church? "Jesus, make your presence known among your people once again."

Let that prayer be introduced early on as you get together with your prayer partner. Let *maranatha* become the grass roots cry of the church all across North America. "Lord Jesus, come again in the clouds or in the church. Either way is fantastic as far as we're concerned!"

Then let us all rejoice when God answers and gives us the very desires of our heart...*and His.*

Notes

1. *America's Great Revivals* (Minneapolis: Dimension Books, Bethany Fellowship, Inc., n.d.), 27.

2. Fred W. Hoffman, *Revival Times in America* (Boston: W.A. Wilde Co., 1956), 76-77.

3. J. Edwin Orr, *The Eager Feet: Evangelical Awakenings, 1790-1830* (Chicago: Moody Press, 1975), 63.

4. J. Edwin Orr, *The Light of the Nations* (Grand Rapids: Eerdmans, 1965), 103-105.

5. Ibid., 105.

6. *America's Great Revivals*, 65-66.

Work Sheet D

Use the following pages to list what you perceive Christ's prayer requests might be. Do this on your own and/or brainstorm ideas with your prayer partner(s). The "Reference Point" column is for notes such as the reason you believe the item concerns the Lord. You might even categorize each request listed (i.e. for believers in general, regarding our local church, concerning spiritual leaders, etc.)

What I/we perceive might be some of Christ's prayer requests	Reference Point: (Why? Scripture rationale? Category? Date? etc.)
Examples: • *That all who believe may be brought to unity.* • *That our church will develop a greater sense of caring and compassion within the body.* • *For mature leaders*	*John 17:20* • *For believers in general* *Phil. 2:1-4* • *Regarding our local church.* *Titus 1:6-9* • *Let these matters be true regarding the leadership at our church… began praying in Oct. '91.*

Work Sheet E

Christ's Prayer Requests	Reference Point

Work Sheet F

Christ's Prayer Requests	Reference Point

Work Sheet G

Christ's Prayer Requests	Reference Point

Work Sheet H

The following pages are designed to help you think through areas in your life about which you need to pray. Under each category listed make notes of specifics you should take before the Lord. Hopefully, as time passes, you'll feel free to share many of these items with your prayer partner(s) and learn to benefit from their support and encouragement as you spend time together in the presence of Christ.

SPOUSE	
Needs	Results Desired

Work Sheet I

CHILDREN	
Needs	Results Desired

EXTENDED FAMILY (include in-laws)	
Needs	Results Desired

Work Sheet J

CHURCH RELATIONSHIPS	
Needs	Results Desired
WORK RELATIONSHIPS	
Needs	Results Desired

Work Sheet K

FRIENDS	
Needs	Results Desired

NEIGHBORS	
Needs	Results Desired

Work Sheet L

COMMUNITY CONCERNS	
Needs	Results Desired
NATIONAL CONCERNS	
Needs	Results Desired

Work Sheet M

WORLD CONCERNS	
Needs	Results Desired

OVERSEAS MISSIONS	
Needs	Results Desired

Work Sheet N

PERSONAL CONCERNS	
Needs	Results Desired
Spiritual Disciplines:	
Physical Health Disciplines:	
Troubling Temptations:	
Ministry Opportunities:	

Work Sheet O

PERSONAL CONCERNS (Continued)	
Needs	Results Desired
Vocational Goals:	
Dreams:	
ADDITIONAL CONCERNS	
Needs	Results Desired

Work Sheet P

KEEPING RECORDS OVER TIME
WILL BUILD YOUR FAITH!

The following pages are for you and your prayer partner(s) to record God's involvement in your lives:

Date Shared	Prayers Requests	Date Answered

Work Sheet Q

Date Shared	Prayer Requests	Date Answered

Work Sheet R

Date Shared	Prayer Requests	Date Answered

Work Sheet S

Date Shared	Prayer Requests	Date Answered

Selected Prayer Passages

Preparing for Prayer through Praise and Thanksgiving

Give thanks to the LORD, call on his name; make known among the nations what he has done. Sing to him, sing praise to him; tell of all his wonderful acts. Glory in his holy name; let the hearts of those who seek the LORD rejoice. Look to the LORD and his strength; seek his face always (1 Chronicles 16:8-11).

I will praise you, O LORD, with all my heart; I will tell of all your wonders. I will be glad and rejoice in you; I will sing praise to your name, O Most High (Psalm 9:1-2).

I will sing to the LORD, for he has been good to me (Psalm 13:6).

I call to the LORD, who is worthy of praise, and I am saved from my enemies (Psalm 18:3).

Therefore I will praise you among the nations, O LORD; I will sing praises to your name (Psalm 18:49).

Ascribe to the LORD the glory due his name; worship the LORD in the splendor of his holiness (Psalm 29:2).

Rejoice in the LORD and be glad, you righteous; sing, all you who are upright in heart! (Psalm 32:11).

I will extol the LORD at all times; his praise will always be on my lips (Psalm 34:1).

My tongue will speak of your righteousness and of your praises all day long (Psalm 35:28).

He put a new song in my mouth, a hymn of praise to our God. Many will see and fear and put their trust in the LORD (Psalm 40:3).

I will praise you forever for what you have done; in your name I will hope, for your name is good. I will praise you in the presence of your saints (Psalm 52:9).

Because your love is better than life, my lips will glorify you. I will praise you as long as I live, and in your name I will lift up my hands (Psalm 63:3-4).

Praise be to the Lord, to God our Savior, who daily bears our burdens (Psalm 68:19).

I will praise God's name in song and glorify him with thanksgiving (Psalm 69:30).

My mouth is filled with your praise, declaring your splendor all day long (Psalm 71:8).

Then we your people, the sheep of your pasture, will praise you forever; from generation to generation we will recount your praise (Psalm 79:13).

Shout for joy to the LORD, all the earth. Worship the LORD with gladness; come before him with joyful songs. Know that the LORD is God. It is he who made us, and we are his; we are his people, the sheep of his pasture. Enter his gates with thanksgiving and his courts with praise; give thanks to him and praise his name. For the LORD is good and his love endures forever; his faithfulness continues through all generations (Psalm 100).

From the rising of the sun to the place where it sets, the name of the LORD is to be praised (Psalm 113:3).

I will sacrifice a thank offering to you and call on the name of the LORD (Psalm 116:17).

I will exalt you, my God the King; I will praise your name for ever and ever. Every day I will praise you and extol your name for ever and ever. Great is the LORD and most worthy of praise; his greatness no one can fathom (Psalm 145:1-3).

Praise the LORD. Praise God in his sanctuary; praise him in his mighty heavens. Praise him for his acts of power; praise him for his surpassing greatness. Praise him with the sounding of the trumpet, praise him with the harp and lyre, praise him with tambourine and dancing, praise him with the strings and flute, praise him with the clash of cymbals, praise him with resounding cymbals. Let everything that has breath praise the LORD. Praise the LORD (Psalm 150:1-6).

O LORD, you are my God; I will exalt you and praise your name, for in perfect faithfulness you have done marvelous things, things planned long ago (Isaiah 25:1).

Oh, the depth of the riches of the wisdom and knowledge of God! How unsearchable his judgments, and his paths beyond tracing out! "Who has known the mind of the Lord? Or who has been his counselor? Who has ever given to God, that God should repay him?" For from him and through him and to him are all things. To him be the glory forever! Amen (Romans 11:33-36).

Speak to one another with psalms, hymns and spiritual songs. Sing and make music in your heart to the Lord, always giving thanks to God the Father for everything, in the name of our Lord Jesus Christ (Ephesians 5:19-20).

Give thanks in all circumstances, for this is God's will for you in Christ Jesus (1 Thessalonians 5:18).

Now to the King eternal, immortal, invisible, the only God, be honor and glory for ever and ever. Amen (1 Timothy 1:17).

Through Jesus, therefore, let us continually offer to God a sacrifice of praise—the fruit of lips that confess his name (Hebrews 13:15).

"Holy, holy, holy is the Lord God Almighty, who was, and is, and is to come"... "You are worthy, our Lord and God, to receive glory and honor and power, for you created all things, and by your will they were created and have their being" (Revelation 4:8b,11).

In a loud voice they sang: "Worthy is the Lamb, who was slain, to receive power and wealth and wisdom and strength and honor and glory and praise!" Then I heard every creature in heaven and on earth and under the earth and on the sea, and all that is in them, singing: "To him who sits on the throne and to the Lamb be praise and honor and glory and power, for ever and ever!" (Revelation 5:12-13).

Finding Confidence in the Promises of God

Be strong and courageous. Do not be afraid or terrified because of them, for the LORD your God goes with you; he will never leave you nor forsake you (Deuteronomy 31:6).

For the sake of his great name the LORD will not reject his people, because the LORD was pleased to make you his own (1 Samuel 12:22).

But let all who take refuge in you be glad; let them ever sing for joy. Spread your protection over them, that those who love your name may rejoice in you (Psalm 5:11).

Those who know your name will trust in you, for you, LORD, have never forsaken those who seek you (Psalm 9:10).

I will be glad and rejoice in your love, for you saw my affliction and knew the anguish of my soul (Psalm 31:7).

A righteous man may have many troubles, but the LORD delivers him from them all (Psalm 34:19).

Why are you downcast, O my soul? Why so disturbed within me? Put your hope in God, for I will yet praise him, my Savior and my God (Psalm 42:11).

Cast your cares on the LORD and he will sustain you; he will never let the righteous fall (Psalm 55:22).

In God, whose word I praise, in God I trust; I will not be afraid. What can mortal man do to me? (Psalm 56:4).

"Because he loves me," says the LORD, "I will rescue him; I will protect him, for he acknowledges my name. He will call upon me, and I will answer him; I will be with him in trouble, I will deliver him and honor him" (Psalm 91:14-15).

I lift up my eyes to the hills—where does my help come from? My help comes from the LORD, the Maker of heaven and earth (Psalm 121:1-2).

Though I walk in the midst of trouble, you preserve my life; you stretch out your hand against the anger of my foes, with your right hand you save me (Psalm 138:7).

The LORD is near to all who call on him, to all who call on him in truth. He fulfills the desires of those who fear him; he hears their cry and saves them (Psalm 145:18-19).

For the LORD will be your confidence and will keep your foot from being snared (Proverbs 3:26).

The LORD is far from the wicked but he hears the prayer of the righteous (Proverbs 15:29).

Surely God is my salvation; I will trust and not be afraid. The LORD, the LORD, is my strength and my song; he has become my salvation (Isaiah 12:2).

This is what the Sovereign LORD, the Holy One of Israel, says: "In repentance and rest is your salvation, in quietness and trust is your strength, but you would have none of it" (Isaiah 30:15).

But those who hope in the L*ORD* will renew their strength. They will soar on wings like eagles; they will run and not grow weary, they will walk and not be faint (Isaiah 40:31).

So do not fear, for I am with you; do not be dismayed, for I am your God. I will strengthen you and help you; I will uphold you with my righteous right hand (Isaiah 41:10).

When you pass through the waters, I will be with you; and when you pass through the rivers, they will not sweep over you. When you walk through the fire, you will not be burned; the flames will not set you ablaze (Isaiah 43:2).

Before they call I will answer; while they are still speaking I will hear (Isaiah 65:24).

The L*ORD* is good, a refuge in times of trouble. He cares for those who trust in him (Nahum 1:7).

So he said to me, "This is the word of the L*ORD* to Zerubbabel: 'Not by might nor by power, but by my Spirit,' says the L*ORD* Almighty" (Zechariah 4:6).

Again, I tell you that if two of you on earth agree about anything you ask for, it will be done for you by my Father in heaven. For where two or three come together in my name, there am I with them (Matthew 18:19).

And surely I am with you always, to the very end of the age (Matthew 28:20b).

Do not let your hearts be troubled. Trust in God; trust also in me (John 14:1).

I tell you the truth, anyone who has faith in me will do what I have been doing. He will do even greater things than these, because I am going to the Father. And I will do whatever you ask in my name, so that the Son may bring glory to the Father (John 14:12-13).

If you remain in me and my words remain in you, ask whatever you wish, and it will be given you (John 15:7).

In that day you will no longer ask me anything. I tell you the truth, my Father will give you whatever you ask in my name (John 16:23).

And we know that in all things God works for the good of those who love him, who have been called according to his purpose (Romans 8:28).

Who shall separate us from the love of Christ? Shall trouble or hardship or persecution or famine or nakedness or danger or sword? As it is written: "For your sake we face death all day long; we are considered as sheep to be slaughtered." No, in all these things we are more than conquerors through him who loved us. For I am convinced that neither death nor life, neither angels nor demons, neither the present nor the future, nor any powers, neither height nor depth, nor anything else in all creation, will be able to separate us from the love of God that is in Christ Jesus our Lord (Romans 8:35-39).

No temptation has seized you except what is common to man. And God is faithful; he will not let you be tempted beyond what you can bear. But when you are tempted, he will also provide a way out so that you can stand up under it (1 Corinthians 10:13).

Praise be to the God and Father of our Lord Jesus Christ, the Father of compassion and the God of all comfort, who comforts us in all our troubles, so that we can comfort those in any trouble with the comfort we ourselves have received from God (2 Corinthians 1:3-4).

We are hard pressed on every side, but not crushed; perplexed, but not in despair; persecuted, but not abandoned; struck down, but not destroyed (2 Corinthians 4:8-9).

In all my prayers for all of you, I always pray with joy because of your partnership in the gospel from the first day until now, being confident of this, that he who began a good work in you will carry it on to completion until the day of Christ Jesus (Philippians 1:4-6).

Do not be anxious about anything, but in everything, by prayer and petition, with thanksgiving, present your requests to God. And the peace of God, which transcends all understanding, will guard your hearts and your minds in Christ Jesus (Philippians 4:6-7).

I know what it is to be in need, and I know what it is to have plenty. I have learned the secret of being content in any and every situation, whether well fed or hungry, whether living in plenty or in want. I can do everything through him who gives me strength (Philippians 4:12-13).

Therefore, since we have a great high priest who has gone through the heavens, Jesus the Son of God, let us hold firmly to the faith we profess. For we do not have a high priest who is unable to sympathize with our weaknesses, but we have one who has been tempted in every way, just as we are—yet was without sin. Let us then approach the throne of grace with confidence, so that we may receive mercy and find grace to help us in our time of need (Hebrews 4:14-16).

So do not throw away your confidence; it will be richly rewarded. You need to persevere so that when you have done the will of God, you will receive what he has promised (Hebrews 10:35-36).

Come near to God and he will come near to you. Wash your hands, you sinners, and purify your hearts, you double-minded (James 4:8).

Cast all your anxiety on him because he cares for you (1 Peter 5:7).

The Lord is not slow in keeping his promise, as some understand slowness. He is patient with you, not wanting anyone to perish, but everyone to come to repentance (2 Peter 3:9).

Dear friends, if our hearts do not condemn us, we have confidence before God (1 John 3:21).

You, dear children, are from God and have overcome them, because the one who is in you is greater than the one who is in the world (1 John 4:4).

This is the confidence we have in approaching God: that if we ask anything according to his will, he hears us. And if we know that he hears us—whatever we ask—we know that we have what we asked of him (1 John 5:14-15).

Seeking God's Wisdom and Direction

Lead me, O LORD, in your righteousness because of my enemies—make straight your way before me (Psalm 5:8).

I will praise the LORD, who counsels me; even at night my heart instructs me. I have set the LORD always before me. Because he is at my right hand, I will not be shaken (Psalm 16:7-8).

You have made known to me the path of life; you will fill me with joy in your presence, with eternal pleasures at your right hand (Psalm 16:11).

As for God, his way is perfect; the word of the LORD is flawless. He is a shield for all who take refuge in him (Psalm 18:30).

Guide me in your truth and teach me, for you are God my Savior, and my hope is in you all day long (Psalm 25:5).

He guides the humble in what is right and teaches them his way (Psalm 25:9).

Teach me your way, O LORD; lead me in a straight path because of my oppressors (Psalm 27:11).

Wait for the LORD; be strong and take heart and wait for the LORD (Psalm 27:14).

We wait in hope for the LORD; he is our help and our shield (Psalm 33:20).

Trust in the LORD and do good; dwell in the land and enjoy safe pasture. Delight yourself in the LORD and he will give you the desires of your heart. Commit your way to the LORD; trust in him and he will do this: He will make your righteousness shine like the dawn, the justice of your cause like the noonday sun. Be still before the LORD and wait patiently for him; do not fret when men succeed in their ways, when they carry out their wicked schemes (Psalm 37:3-7).

For this God is our God for ever and ever; he will be our guide even to the end (Psalm 48:14).

Call upon me in the day of trouble; I will deliver you, and you will honor me (Psalm 50:15).

Then my enemies will turn back when I call for help. By this I will know that God is for me (Psalm 56:9).

Find rest, O my soul, in God alone; my hope comes from him (Psalm 62:5).

Trust in him at all times, O people; pour out your hearts to him, for God is our refuge (Psalm 62:8).

You guide me with your counsel, and afterward you will take me into glory (Psalm 73:24).

[God] satisfies your desires with good things so that your youth is renewed like the eagle's (Psalm 103:5).

Teach me, O Lord, to follow your decrees; then I will keep them to the end (Psalm 119:33).

Your word is a lamp to my feet and a light for my path (Psalm 119:105).

The LORD will fulfill his purpose for me; your love, O LORD, endures forever—do not abandon the works of your hands (Psalm 138:8).

Search me, O God, and know my heart; test me and know my anxious thoughts. See if there is any offensive way in me, and lead me in the way everlasting (Psalm 139:23-24).

Teach me to do your will, for you are my God; may your good Spirit lead me on level ground (Psalm 143:10).

The eyes of all look to you, and you give them their food at the proper time. You open your hand and satisfy the desires of every living thing (Psalm 145:15-16).

Trust in the LORD with all your heart and lean not on your own understanding; in all your ways acknowledge him, and he will make your paths straight (Proverbs 3:5-6).

The lot is cast into the lap, but its every decision is from the LORD (Proverbs 16:33).

A man's steps are directed by the LORD. How then can anyone understand his own way? (Proverbs 20:24)

In that day they will say, "Surely this is our God; we trusted in him, and he saved us.

This is the LORD, we trusted in him; let us rejoice and be glad in his salvation" (Isaiah 25:9).

But those who hope in the LORD will renew their strength. They will soar on wings like eagles; they will run and not grow weary, they will walk and not be faint (Isaiah 40:31).

I will lead the blind by ways they have not known, along unfamiliar paths I will guide them; I will turn the darkness into light before them and make the rough places smooth. These are the things I will do; I will not forsake them (Isaiah 42:16).

"For my thoughts are not your thoughts, neither are your ways my ways," declares the LORD. "As the heavens are higher than the earth, so are my ways higher than your ways and my thoughts than your thoughts" (Isaiah 55:8-9).

Call to me and I will answer you and tell you great and unsearchable things you do not know (Jeremiah 33:3).

Let us acknowledge the LORD; let us press on to acknowledge him. As surely as the sun rises, he will appear; he will come to us like the winter rains, like the spring rains that water the earth (Hosea 6:3).

Ask and it will be given to you; seek and you will find; knock and the door will be opened to you. For everyone who asks receives; he who seeks finds; and to him who knocks, the door will be opened (Matthew 7:7-8).

If you believe, you will receive whatever you ask for in prayer (Matthew 21:22).

Therefore I tell you, whatever you ask for in prayer, believe that you have received it, and it will be yours (Mark 11:24).

What, then, shall we say in response to this? If God is for us, who can be against us? (Romans 8:31)

We have come to share in Christ if we hold firmly till the end the confidence we had at first (Hebrews 3:14).

Let us then approach the throne of grace with confidence, so that we may receive mercy and find grace to help us in our time of need (Hebrews 4:16).

Let us hold unswervingly to the hope we profess, for he who promised is faithful (Hebrews 10:23).

Developing a
Prayerful Attitude

But if from there you seek the LORD your
God, you will find him if you look for him
with all your heart and with all your soul
(Deuteronomy 4:29).

If my people, who are called by my name,
will humble themselves and pray and seek
my face and turn from their wicked ways,
then will I hear from heaven and will forgive their sin and will heal their land
(2 Chronicles 7:14).

You hear, O LORD, the desire of the af-
flicted; you encourage them, and you listen
to their cry (Psalm 10:17).

Keep your servant also from willful sins;
may they not rule over me. Then will I be

blameless, innocent of great transgression. May the words of my mouth and the meditation of my heart be pleasing in your sight, O LORD, my Rock and my Redeemer (Psalm 19:13-14).

The earth is the LORD's, and everything in it, the world, and all who live in it; for he founded it upon the seas and established it upon the waters. Who may ascend the hill of the LORD? Who may stand in his holy place? He who has clean hands and a pure heart, who does not lift up his soul to an idol or swear by what is false. He will receive blessing from the LORD and vindication from God his Savior. Such is the generation of those who seek him, who seek your face, O God of Jacob (Psalm 24:1-6).

Vindicate me, O LORD, for I have led a blameless life; I have trusted in the LORD without wavering. Test me, O LORD, and try me, examine my heart and my mind (Psalm 26:1-2).

Then my soul will rejoice in the LORD and delight in his salvation (Psalm 35:9).

Create in me a pure heart, O God, and renew a steadfast spirit within me. Do not cast me from your presence or take your Holy Spirit from me. Restore to me the joy of your salvation and grant me a willing spirit, to sustain me. Then I will teach transgressors your ways, and sinners will turn back to you (Psalm 51:10-13).

If I had cherished sin in my heart, the Lord would not have listened; but God has surely listened and heard my voice in prayer (Psalm 66:18-19).

Search me, O God, and know my heart; test me and know my anxious thoughts. See if there is any offensive way in me, and lead me in the way everlasting (Psalm 139:23-24).

The LORD is far from the wicked but he hears the prayer of the righteous (Proverbs 15:29).

"Woe to me!" I cried. "I am ruined! For I am a man of unclean lips, and I live among a people of unclean lips, and my eyes have seen the King, the LORD Almighty" (Isaiah 6:5).

For this is what the high and lofty One says—he who lives forever, whose name is holy: "I live in a high and holy place, but also with him who is contrite and lowly in spirit, to revive the spirit of the lowly and to revive the heart of the contrite (Isaiah 57:15).

You will seek me and find me when you seek me with all your heart (Jeremiah 29:13).

He has showed you, O man, what is good. And what does the LORD require of you? To act justly and to love mercy and to walk humbly with your God (Micah 6:8).

Not everyone who says to me, "Lord, Lord," will enter the kingdom of heaven, but only he who does the will of my Father who is in heaven (Matthew 7:21).

And when you stand praying, if you hold anything against anyone, forgive him, so that your Father in heaven may forgive you your sins (Mark 11:25).

If you obey my commands, you will remain in my love, just as I have obeyed my Father's commands and remain in his love (John 15:10).

Since we have these promises, dear friends, let us purify ourselves from everything that contaminates body and spirit, perfecting holiness out of reverence for God (2 Corinthians 7:1).

And this is my prayer: that your love may abound more and more in knowledge and depth of insight, so that you may be able to discern what is best and may be pure and blameless until the day of Christ (Philippians 1:9-10).

Bear with each other and forgive whatever grievances you may have against one another. Forgive as the Lord forgave you (Colossians 3:13).

For I will forgive their wickedness and will remember their sins no more (Hebrews 8:12).

Humble yourselves before the Lord, and he will lift you up (James 4:10).

For the eyes of the Lord are on the righteous and his ears are attentive to their prayer, but the face of the Lord is against those who do evil (1 Peter 3:12).

My dear children, I write this to you so that you will not sin. But if anybody does sin, we have one who speaks to the Father in our defense—Jesus Christ, the Righteous One (1 John 2:1).

[We] receive from him anything we ask, because we obey his commands and do what pleases him (1 John 3:22).

To him who is able to keep you from falling and to present you before his glorious presence without fault and with great joy—to the only God our Savior be glory, majesty, power and authority, through Jesus Christ our Lord, before all ages, now and forevermore! Amen (Jude 24-25).